# ANGRY PARENT ANGRY CHILD

## WORKBOOK

Your 4-Week Guided Workbook to Stop Yelling, Manage Anger, and Build a Calmer Connection with Your Child

Carrie Khang

| Angry Parent Angry Child | 4-week guide Workbook |
| --- | --- |

# Contents

# Introduction

Hey there, fellow parent on the quest for calm (and maybe just five minutes of silence).

Before we begin, take a breath. Parenting is hard—not because you're doing it wrong, but because it's just hard. You're raising tiny humans with their own feelings, needs, and storms. And you're trying to guide them while carrying your own.

This workbook isn't here to turn you into the perfect parent. Your child doesn't need perfect. They just need you. The real you. The one who gets it wrong, apologizes, tries again, and keeps showing up with love.

Over the next 28 days, we'll explore anger, yelling, guilt, and all the hidden stress of parenting. But this isn't about shame or judgment. It's about understanding why you react the way you do, and how to respond differently. It's definitely about learning new skills, but more importantly, it's about seeing your anger as a signal, not a failure.

You'll find simple reflections and tiny daily actions in this workbook that bring real change over time—not the kind that promises a magically peaceful house overnight, but the kind that grows strong roots so you and your child can weather life's storms together.

So, pour your coffee (even if it's gone cold again), find a quiet spot if you can, and settle in. You're not here to "fix" yourself. You're here to get to know yourself better. You're not here to control your child. You're here to connect with them more deeply.

Let's walk these next 28 days together with honesty, courage, and maybe a little laughter along the way. Parenting isn't about getting it right every time. It's about showing up, even when it's messy, tired, and hard.

Here's to showing up human, imperfect, and stronger than you realize. ✦

## MY OATH

Make a promise in your heart and sign the document below.

I, _________________ (your name), pledge to be the parent I aspire
to be, even when I feel lost and uncertain. I love my child(ren),
___________________________________ (name/s of your child/ren), and I
commit to grow alongside them with each passing day.

Whatever I learn from this workbook, I will apply it to myself and
my family. Although there will be challenges and setbacks, I promise
not to give up. I'll continue to learn and make the most of this time.

I'll stay true to my values, express my needs, and keep an open heart
and mind. Through laughter and love, I'll seek the silver linings and
embrace the wonderful chaos of parenting.

My love for my children will guide me to create a nurturing and
harmonious home.


_______________________________

(Signature)

# Week 1

## Understanding Parental Anger

# Day 1: What is Parental Anger?

☑ Insight: Understanding Parental Anger–Your Power to Change

You know that moment—the rising heat, the sudden tension in your chest—when your child pushes one more boundary and you feel yourself starting to snap? You're not alone.

**Parental anger is incredibly common and deeply human.** It's not a sign of failure or weakness. It's not a character flaw. It's a signal that your mind and body are asking for attention, support, or a break. The problem isn't anger itself, but when it becomes a recurring pattern, it can impact how safe, seen, and supported your child feels.

Anger in parenting often stems from layers beneath the surface:

- Built-up stress
- Hidden expectations you didn't know you were holding
- Emotional baggage from your own childhood
- Moments where you feel powerless or invisible

This workbook isn't about "fixing" you—it's about "freeing" you. <u>You're not here to eliminate anger (that would be unrealistic and unhealthy), but to understand it.</u> When you start seeing anger as a signal—not an enemy—you begin reclaiming your power. You become the calm in your child's storm, rather than a storm of your own.

<u>Understanding anger is important.</u> And it will change not only your parenting, but your entire emotional legacy.

## ✏️ Self-Reflection Exercise: Understand Your Anger

Let today be about honesty and not guilt. This is your space to observe with kindness.

What was happening around you when you last felt irritated or angry at your child? (e.g., chaos, running late, feeling unheard)

_______________________________________________

_______________________________________________

What did your body feel like? (e.g., tight chest, clenched jaw, racing heart)

_______________________________________________

_______________________________________________

What did you really need at that moment? (e.g., rest, help, quiet, feeling appreciated)

_______________________________________________

_______________________________________________

What do you think your child needed in that moment? (e.g., connection, clear instruction, comfort)

_______________________________________________

_______________________________________________

One thing you want to remember about anger after today. (e.g., *"It's a signal, not a failure."*)

_______________________________________________

_______________________________________________

## ✎ Understanding Your Anger Style:

How does your parental anger usually express itself? (Check all that apply.)

☐ Yelling more than I want to

☐ Using threats or punishments that I regret later

☐ Feeling emotionally out of control

☐ Withdrawing or giving silent treatment

☐ Feeling guilt or shame after reacting

☐ Experiencing physical tension (tight chest, clenched jaw, racing heart)

☐ Repeating patterns I saw in my own parents

☐ Getting especially triggered by certain behaviors (backtalk, whining, defiance)

☐ Other:

## 🎯 Today's Actionable Task

Here's your challenge today: **Don't suppress your anger. Don't act on it either. Just observe it.** For the next 5 minutes—or the next moment that irritates you—become a quiet observer of your internal world.

When anger rises, pause and ask yourself "What's really making me angry right now?

___________________________________________

___________________________________________

What triggered it? (e.g., your child's tone, mess, chaos, lack of support)

___________________________________________

___________________________________________

What does it feel like in your body? (e.g., tension in shoulders, shallow breath, hot face)

___________________________________________

___________________________________________

What story are you telling yourself at that moment? (e.g., *"They don't care," "I'm failing," "I do everything, and no one helps me"*)

___________________________________________

___________________________________________

##  End-of-The-Day Reflection

What moment today challenged you the most, and how did you respond?

_______________________________________________

_______________________________________________

_______________________________________________

What's one thing you're proud of, no matter how small?

_______________________________________________

_______________________________________________

What's one insight or feeling you want to carry into tomorrow?

_______________________________________________

_______________________________________________

# Day 2: The Parenting Myths You Believe

✅ Insight: Common Parenting Myths That Fuel Frustration

Do you have parenting myths that you truly believe and apply in your parenting every day? Maybe it's something your mom used to say, or some advice your grandmother gave you. Perhaps it's something you saw on Instagram that sounded wise at the time.

What is that belief for you?

We all carry invisible rules about what parenting "should" look like. Some rules are passed down through generations with love, while others stem from fear, guilt, or social media trends. However, here's the truth: many of these beliefs shape our reactions toward our children, often fueling frustration and anger without us even realizing it.

Let's look at a few common ones:

- **Myth:** Good parents are the ones who are always in control.
  - o **Truth:** Parenting isn't about control; it's about guidance, connection, and resilience.

- **Myth:** If my child doesn't listen immediately, they're being disrespectful.
  - o **Truth:** Kids are still developing emotional regulation and impulse control. Delay doesn't always mean defiance.

- **Myth:** If I don't punish them, they'll walk all over me.
  - o **Truth:** Calm, consistent boundaries that are built on respect teach more than punishment ever will.

- **Myth:** My child's behavior reflects my worth as a parent.
  - o **Truth:** Your child is their own person. Your parenting is measured by how you respond, not by their choices.

These myths turn ordinary challenges—whining, big feelings, testing limits—into perceived personal failures. When we feel like we're failing, anger often steps in to protect us. But the real power lies in questioning these beliefs and replacing them with truth, self-compassion, and clarity.

Today, we begin with exactly that.

## ✏ Self-Reflection Exercise: What Myths Are Driving Your Anger?

Think back to a moment when you felt frustrated or angry with your child. Look beneath the surface, what belief might have been fueling that reaction?

Maybe it was:

- "They should know better."
- "If I don't react strongly, I'm being too soft."
- "Their behavior means I'm doing something wrong."

Write down at least two beliefs that surfaced in those moments of stress.

Parenting Myths I've Believed in:

1. _______________________________________________

2. _______________________________________________

## 🎯 Today's Actionable Task

Choose two of the myths you wrote above and **rewrite them into empowering truths** that align with the calm, connected parent you're becoming.

**Example:**

<u>Lie:</u> If I don't yell, my child won't take me seriously.

<u>Truth:</u> When I stay calm, I show my child how to handle big feelings and helps them trust and respect me.

Now, rewrite your own:

1. Lie:

_______________________________________________

Truth:

_______________________________________________

2. Lie:

_______________________________________________

Truth:

_______________________________________________

## End-of-The-Day Reflection

What belief about parenting felt strongest today?

______________________________________________

______________________________________________

How did it affect the way you showed up for your child?

______________________________________________

______________________________________________

What learning do you want to carry into tomorrow?

______________________________________________

______________________________________________

# Day 3 : Why Are You Angrier Than Other Parents?

 **Insight: Understanding Your Triggers**

Have you ever wondered why you seem to lose your temper more easily than other parents? Maybe you've noticed yourself snapping at your child over small things and have thought, "Why can't I just stay calm like other parents?"

Here is the truth: your anger isn't just about your child's behavior. It often runs much deeper, <u>rooted in your own childhood experiences.</u> For example, think about the ways your parents spoke to you in your childhood. Did they say things like, "You got that from your dad," whenever you made a mistake? Maybe they raised their voice or gave you the silent treatment. Or maybe they used guilt, like "After all I've done for you…"

Maybe you promised yourself you'd never repeat those words, only to hear them coming out of your mouth when your child misbehaved.

Sometimes your anger has roots
deeper than the moment.

Many of us carry <u>unhealed wounds from our childhood into our parenting</u>. We either recreate the patterns we grew up with or try so hard to do the opposite that we overcompensate and react with anger, guilt, or fear.

A Burmese proverb says, "Parents are the first teachers of children."

The way your parents related to you taught you how to relate to the world. This is the case with you and your child as well.

Sometimes, you let anger take over because something your child does triggers your memories, feelings, or values from your own upbringing. These subconscious flashbacks can cause you to overreact before you even realize what's happening.

Triggers can come from:

- Feeling disrespected
- Chronic exhaustion
- Sensory overload
- Being publicly embarrassed
- Repeating the emotional patterns of your childhood

## ✏️ Self-Reflection Exercise: Exploring Your Anger Roots

Take a moment today to reflect honestly:

How have your parents impacted you—positively or negatively?

_______________________________________________

How was anger expressed in your family growing up?

_______________________________________________

_______________________________________________

What phrases or reactions from your parents do you find yourself repeating?

_______________________________________________

_______________________________________________

_______________________________________________

When you were your child's age, how did your parents usually express anger?

_______________________________________________

_______________________________________________

Are you acting or sounding just like your parents in ways you aren't proud of?

_______________________________________________

_______________________________________________

Are you projecting your childhood experiences onto your child?

_______________________________________________

_______________________________________________

Did your parents raise you in ways you never want to recreate with your child?

_______________________________________________

_______________________________________________

Write down whatever comes to your mind. Remember, this is a safe space for honesty without judgment.

_______________________________________________

_______________________________________________

_______________________________________________

## 🎯 Today's Actionable Task

Choose one phrase or reaction from your parents that you notice yourself repeating when you're angry.

**Example:**
**Phrase:** "Stop crying or I'll give you something to cry about."

**Childhood feeling:** Fearful and alone

**Empowering rewrite:** "I see you're upset. Let's take a moment to calm down together."

Now, it's your turn.

Phrase or reaction:

_____________________________________

_____________________________________

How did it make you feel?

_____________________________________

_____________________________________

Your empowering rewrite:

_____________________________________

_____________________________________

## ▉ End-of-The-Day Reflection

What did you learn about yourself today?

_____________________________________________________

_____________________________________________________

_____________________________________________________

How did recognizing your childhood experiences affect the way you showed up for your child?

_____________________________________________________

_____________________________________________________

_____________________________________________________

What intentions do you want to carry into tomorrow to break these cycles with compassion?

_____________________________________________________

_____________________________________________________

# Day 4: What Triggers You the Most?

**Insight: Understanding Your Parenting Triggers**

Yesterday, you explored why you might feel angrier than other parents, uncovering how your childhood experiences and upbringing shaped the way you react with your child.

Today, let's take that self-awareness a step further.

Even when we understand our deeper anger roots, certain moments with our kids can still push our buttons instantly. That's because we all have specific triggers—behaviors, words, tones, or situations that set off a strong emotional reaction in us.

For example, it could be your child's whining tone, their eye-rolling, or when they ignore your instructions. Triggers aren't just about what your child is doing, but how their behavior makes you feel inside.

These triggers often link back to your past, your beliefs, or unmet needs. <u>That's why something small to others can feel huge to you</u>.

Today, we'll identify the top triggers that can set off your anger, frustration, or stress in your parenting. Once you name them, you can begin to create calm, confident responses that align with the parent you want to be.

## ✏️ Self-Reflection Exercise:

Identify Your Top 3 Personal Triggers

Write down your **top 3 triggers** that set off anger, frustration, or stress in your parenting.

Here are some common examples to consider:

- Slow transitions (e.g., getting ready, bedtime, leaving the house)
- Disrespectful tone or eye-rolling
- Incessant crying, whining, or yelling
- Feeling embarrassed by your child's behavior in public
- Comparing your child to others' children
- Feeling taken for granted or unappreciated

Write down your top 3 triggers in parenting.

1. _______________________________________________

2. _______________________________________________

3. _______________________________________________


## ◎ Today's Actionable Task

Choose **one of your triggers** from above and create a simple plan to respond calmly the next time you get triggered.

Example:

**Trigger:** Whining for more snacks after I said no

**Your usual reaction:** Yell "I said NO, stop asking me!"

**New calm response:** Take a breath, get down to their level, and say, "I hear you really want more snacks. I know it's hard to wait until dinner."

Trigger:

_______________________________________________

_______________________________________________


My usual reaction:

_______________________________________________

_______________________________________________

New calm response I will try:

_______________________________________________

_______________________________________________

## End-of-The-Day Reflection

What did you notice about your triggers today?

_______________________________________________

_______________________________________________

How did your new calm response change your interaction with your child?

_______________________________________________

_______________________________________________

What is one intention you want to carry into tomorrow?

_______________________________________________

_______________________________________________

# Day 5: Choosing Your Battles

**✻ Insight: You Don't Have to Win Every Fight**

Imagine installing a CCTV camera in your home and watching yourself parenting all day. You might hear:

- "Do this."
- "Don't do that."
- "Wear this."
- "Stop touching that."
- "Come here."
- "Go there."
- "Come back here."
- "Put this away."
- "Don't say that."

You might not realize it, but you're constantly giving orders and corrections to your child. By bedtime, you're thinking, "Why are my kids so hard to handle?"

Here's the truth: when you fight every battle, you end up exhausted and angry. Your child feels controlled and resists you even more. Parenting becomes a never-ending power struggle.

Choosing your battles means deciding which behaviors are truly worth addressing and which you can let go of. Not every behavior needs correction.

When you let go of small issues and save your energy for what truly matters- their safety, health, and respectful behavior, you create more peace for yourself and your child.

✔️ **Let them win (when it doesn't harm them)**

Allowing your child to win small battles builds their independence and confidence. For example, if they refuse to eat broccoli but eat other vegetables, or insist on wearing the blue shirt instead of the green one- is it really worth the fight today?

✔️ **Fight to win (when it's essential)**

Some battles are non-negotiable for their well-being, such as brushing teeth, bedtime, homework, or respectful words and actions. Your firmness should teach responsibility, not control.

Other situations where you must hold firm include:

- Wearing a helmet when riding a bike.
- Not climbing unsafe places like high bookshelves.
- Using safe hands — no hitting, kicking, or hurting others.

These aren't about control- they're about teaching responsibility, respect, and safety. Your firmness in these areas guides your child's growth, while saving your energy for what truly matters.

Today, you will practice choosing your battles with calmness and clarity instead of anger.

# FIGHT TO WIN
### (when it's essential)

## ✏️ Self-Reflection Exercise:

**What Battles Are You Fighting For?**

Write down **3 common battles** you have with your child each day.

1. ________________________________________________

2. ________________________________________________

3. ________________________________________________

Pick one common battle you often have with your child.

Why does this bother me so much?

_______________________________

_______________________________

_______________________________

How can I either let it go or enforce it calmly?

_______________________________

_______________________________

_______________________________

## ⊙ Today's Actionable Task

Today, choose **1 small battle to let go of without correcting.**

**Example:**

**Let go:** Wearing mismatched socks

Battle to let go:

_______________________________

How will I let it go today without any comment or reaction?

_______________________________

_______________________________

_______________________________

## End-of-The-Day Reflection

What did you notice about yourself when you let go of a small battle today?

_______________________________________________

_______________________________________________

What intention do you want to carry into tomorrow to create a more peaceful home?

_______________________________________________

_______________________________________________

# Day 6: Understanding Power Struggles



### ❋ Insight: Why Do Power Struggles Happen?

A power struggle is akin to an emotional tug-of-war, where winning the argument takes precedence over **solving the problem**.

These battles often start over seemingly small issues—screen time, bedtime, homework—but they escalate when both sides feel unheard, unseen, or disrespected.

You might recognize this moment: your child says "No," you say it louder, their defiance grows, and suddenly the room feels like a battlefield.

The more you push, the more your child pushes back. Soon, you're no longer solving a problem. You're stuck in a loop of control, resistance, and frustration. Your voice gets louder, their behavior becomes more challenging, and everyone ends up angry and disconnected.

Here's the important truth: **Your job isn't to win every fight. Your job is to step out of the struggle so you can guide your child with clarity, not conflict.**

When children resist, it's often a signal that they feel powerless. Ironically, the more control we try to enforce, the more they feel the need to push back.

Breaking this cycle begins with a pause, a breath, and a shift in approach—from domination to connection. Instead of thinking, "How can I make them obey?", start asking, "How can we work together to solve this?"

Power struggles aren't about them defying you. They're about a child needing to feel heard and a parent learning to guide rather than control. Today, you'll learn how to turn battles into opportunities for connection and cooperation.

### 📌 Quick Self-Check:

What Triggers Power Struggles in Your Home? (Check all that apply.)

☐ Homework or chores

☐ Morning or bedtime routines

☐ Screen time limits

☐ Sibling conflicts

☐ Backtalk or attitude

☐ Not following instructions

☐ My child questioning my decisions

☐ Something else: _______________________________________

## ✏️ Self-Reflection Exercise:

**Your Power Struggle Patterns**

Write down one common power struggle you often have with your child:

---

---

What usually triggers this struggle? (Is it their tone, refusal, or your fear of losing control?)

---

How do you feel at that moment? (Angry, powerless, disrespected, anxious?)

---

How do you think your child feels at that moment? (Controlled, scared, unheard, angry?)

---

What might change if you let go of control and focused on connection instead?

---

---

---

## ⌖ Today's Actionable Task

Choose **1 common power struggle** you face. Today, practice stepping out of the tug-of-war by turning a command into a choice and responding with connection.

**Example:**

<u>Command:</u> "Clean up your toys NOW, or I'm throwing them away."

<u>Choice with connection:</u> "I see you're having fun with your toys. Would you like to clean them up now together, or will you do it after dinner?"

Now write your own:

Typical command I give:

__________________________________

__________________________________

New choice-based, connection-focused response:

__________________________________

__________________________________

__________________________________

## ⬛ End-of-the-Day Reflection

How did stepping out of the power struggle change your interaction with your child today?

_______________________________________________

_______________________________________________

_______________________________________________

How did it make you feel as a parent?

_______________________________________________

_______________________________________________

_______________________________________________

What intention do you want to carry into tomorrow to reduce battles and build connection?

_______________________________________________

_______________________________________________

# Day 7: Signs You're an Angry Parent

### ❄ Insight: Why Does Recognizing Your Anger Matter?

Imagine if someone secretly recorded your day with your kids and played it back to you tonight. Would you hear yourself saying:

"STOP IT!"

"WHY CAN'T YOU JUST LISTEN?"

"DO IT NOW!"

Or would you see yourself rolling your eyes, slamming drawers, or sighing loudly in frustration?

We all get angry. But when anger becomes our usual way of communication, our children start walking on eggshells. They become anxious about our reactions instead of learning from our guidance.

Here's the real problem: Most of us don't realize how often anger shows up in our parenting. We think, "It's just discipline," or "They made me angry." But anger is not just about our child's behavior. It's about how overwhelmed, exhausted, disrespected, or powerless we feel in that moment. <u>Anger damages the trust and connection that our children need to thrive.</u>

<u>The goal today is not to shame yourself, but to see your anger clearly. Because what you don't recognize, you can't change.</u>

When you become aware of your anger triggers and patterns, you can start showing up as the calm, strong parent your child truly needs—even on the hardest days.

## ✏️ Self-Reflection Exercise:

**Name It So You Can Change It**

Read through the signs below and check ✓ any that apply to you:

☐ You get angry frequently and yell quickly over small things or minor mistakes.

☐ Your kids seem scared of you. They avoid eye contact or freeze up.

☐ You have a short fuse. You yell suddenly or over minor mistakes.

☐ You have no patience. You lose it when your child is slow or distracted.

☐ You blame your child. You say, "Why do you always make me angry?"

☐ Your kids say you're angry. They ask, "Why do you always yell at me?"

☐ You hold grudges. You stay cold or distant after their mistakes.

Which sign feels most relatable to you right now? Why?

_______________________________________________

_______________________________________________

_______________________________________________

How do you think your anger affects your child emotionally and mentally?

_______________________________________________

_______________________________________________

_______________________________________________

How does it affect your relationship with them long term?

_______________________________________________

_______________________________________________

_______________________________________________

What is one reason behind your anger that has nothing to do with your child's behavior? (Stress, exhaustion, childhood patterns, feeling unappreciated?)

_______________________________________________

_______________________________________________

_______________________________________________

## 🎯 Today's Actionable Task

Choose one situation today where you usually react with anger. When it happens, pause for 5 seconds before you speak or act.

**Example:**

- **<u>Situation:</u>** My child leaves their toys all over the floor.
- **<u>My usual reaction:</u>** "How many times do I have to tell you? Clean up now!"
- **<u>New calm approach:</u>** Pause. Breathe. Remind yourself, "Children are here to learn, and I am here to teach them calmly." Then say, "I see toys everywhere. Let's pick them up together so we can keep our space safe."

**Remember:** Kids learn through calm, repeated guidance, not angry reactions.

Write your plan:

Trigger situation:

_______________________________________________

_______________________________________________

My usual reaction:

_______________________________________________

_______________________________________________

My new calm response:

_______________________________________________

_______________________________________________

## End-of-The-Day Reflection

What did you notice about your anger today?

_______________________________________________

_______________________________________________

What intention do you want to carry into tomorrow to become a calmer parent?

_______________________________________________

_______________________________________________

# Week 2

# Who Owns the Problem? You Or Your Child?

# Day 8: Why Do Children Misbehave

**Insight: Misbehavior Is a Skill Gap—Not a Character Flaw**

When your child screams in the grocery store, hits their sibling, or shouts "I hate you," it can feel like they're being intentionally bad or disrespectful. But here's what many parents don't realize:

Misbehavior isn't usually about being naughty; <u>it's about lacking emotional or social skills</u> <u>or feeling overwhelmed</u>.

Adults and kids aren't so different. <u>Both want to feel good and feel loved</u>. But unlike adults, children don't yet have the words or emotional skills to express what's really going on inside.

**Example:**

- A child who throws a tantrum because they didn't get a toy isn't being bad—they're overwhelmed by disappointment and don't know how to manage it.
- A child who refuses to do homework may feel anxious about failing or embarrassed if they don't understand it.
- A child who hits their sibling might feel jealous, left out, or unable to express big feelings with words.

When you see misbehavior as a message rather than defiance, everything changes. Instead of asking, "Why are they doing this to me?", start asking, "What is making this so hard for them right now?"

**A Practical Parenting Tip:**

Instead of scolding, threatening, or yelling, teach them exactly what to do or give them a meaningful role.

**Example:** Grocery Store Tantrums

If your child runs around or begs for candy:

- **Calmly explain:** "Running here can block other people. It's important to walk safely in stores."
- **Involve them:** "Can you help me pick out the yogurt you like? Can you find the apples for us?"
- **Offer them choices to redirect behavior:** "You can sit in the cart or walk next to me. You choose."

Giving children clear guidance, small responsibilities, and simple choices helps them feel capable and reduces power struggles.

## ✏ Self-Reflection Exercise:

**Looking Beneath the Behavior**

Think about the past day or week. Write down one moment when your child misbehaved:

What exactly happened?

_______________________________________________

_______________________________________________

What do you think was really going on underneath their behavior? (Were they tired, hungry, overwhelmed, feeling disconnected, lacking a skill?)

_______________________________________________

_______________________________________________

How did you react in that moment?

_______________________________________________

_______________________________________________

If you had viewed their behavior as communication, what might you have done differently?

_______________________________________________

_______________________________________________

## ◎ Today's Actionable Task

Today, when your child misbehaves, pause and ask yourself:

- "What is my child trying to tell me right now?"
- "What feeling or struggle is underneath this behavior?"

**Example:**

**Situation:** Your child whines and cries about brushing their teeth.

**Old response:** "Stop whining and just do it now!"

**New response:** Pause. Think, "They might be tired or overwhelmed." Then say calmly, "I see you're tired. Do you want to brush your teeth by yourself, or would you like my help tonight?"

Giving them a simple choice teaches them they still have control while learning what needs to be done.

Now write your plan:

A likely behavior of your child you'll see today:

__________________________________________

__________________________________________

New question you'll ask yourself:

__________________________________________

__________________________________________

New calm, supportive response:

_______________________________________

_______________________________________

## End-of-The-Day Reflection

What did you notice about your child's behavior today when you viewed it as communication?

_______________________________________

_______________________________________

What intention do you want to carry into tomorrow to keep practicing this mindset shift?

_______________________________________

_______________________________________

# Day 9: All Behavior Is Communication



## ❄ Insight: All Behavior Is Communication

Sometimes it feels like your child's behavior is designed to push your buttons. They whine when you're tired. They shout "No!" when you're in a rush. They argue about everything.

It can feel personal, like they're deliberately trying to make your day harder. But here's a truth I keep reminding you of in this book because it's so important to accept:

Your child is not someone you punish for struggling; <u>they're someone to teach with patience. Children are learning every single day. They need parents who see them as students of life, not as problems to fix.</u>

Yes, it's hard not to say, "How many times do I have to tell you this?" especially when you're exhausted. But each time you calmly teach them what to do, you build their skills and show them that love does not depend on perfection.

<u>All behavior is communication.</u> It's not that their behavior is acceptable, but it's understandable when you see it as a message rather than defiance. Their actions are telling you, <u>"I need help learning how to handle this better."</u>

Children aren't born knowing how to say:

- "I feel overwhelmed."
- "I'm tired and hungry."
- "I feel disconnected from you today."
- "I'm scared you're mad at me."

Instead, they show it through their actions, whining, tantrums, defiance, clinging, or acting out. These are their ways of communicating their needs they can't yet express with words.

Think about it:

- Adults say, "I've had a stressful day at work."
- Children throw toys, slam doors, or scream.

**Remember:** <u>Your child isn't giving you a hard time. They're having a hard time and showing it the only way they know how to right now.</u>

## ✏️ Self-Reflection Exercise:

**Listening to the Message Beneath Your Child's Behavior**

Think about a recent moment when you tried to correct your child.

What was their behavior? (e.g., refusing to listen, shouting, ignoring you, slamming doors)

________________________________________________________

________________________________________________________

What do you think they were really trying to communicate? (e.g., feeling tired, wanting control, needing attention, feeling anxious)

________________________________________________________

________________________________________________________

How did you respond in that moment?

________________________________________________________

________________________________________________________

If you viewed this behavior as communication, how could you respond differently the next time to teach them calmly while also holding your boundary?

________________________________________________________

________________________________________________________

## 🎯 Today's Actionable Task

Today, when your child behaves in a way that frustrates you, pause and ask yourself:

"<u>My job is to teach them, not punish them</u>."

Then ask:

"What is my child trying to say from this behavior?"

<u>Instead of reacting immediately, respond to the message behind the behavior.</u>

**Example:**

**<u>Behavior:</u>** Your child yells "I hate you!" when you say no to more TV.

**<u>Old response:</u>** "Don't you dare talk to me like that!"

**<u>New response:</u>** Pause. Think, "They're upset and disappointed." Then say calmly, "I hear you're really angry about the TV turning off. It's okay to feel mad, but it's not okay to say hurtful words."

Now write your plan:

Your child's behavior that you might see today:

_______________________________________________

_______________________________________________

What might they be communicating?

_______________________________________________

_______________________________________________

Your new calm, understanding response to their behavior.

_______________________________________________

_______________________________________________

_______________________________________________

## End-of-The-Day Reflection

What did you notice about your child's behavior when you saw it as communication?

_______________________________________________

_______________________________________________

How did this change your reaction and their response?

_______________________________________________

_______________________________________________

What intention do you want to carry into tomorrow to keep practicing this mindset shift?

_______________________________________________

_______________________________________________

## Day 10: You're Bad at Interpretations

 **Insight: Why Do You Often Jump to Negative Interpretations?**

Think about the last time your child didn't listen to you, whined, or refused to follow your instructions. Did you immediately think:

- "They're being disrespectful."
- "They're doing this to push my buttons."
- "They never listen because they don't care about what I say."

We often jump straight to **negative interpretations of our child's behavior**. But why?

Because these interpretations come from **fear and insecurity**:

- Fear that you're failing as a parent
- Fear that your child will "turn out bad" if you don't correct them immediately
- Insecurity about not feeling respected or in control

Here's the truth: **Kids are kids. Their brains aren't fully developed yet.**

They're not trying to make your life hard—they're just doing things the way kids do.

Children's brains, especially the parts responsible for impulse control, empathy, and thinking ahead, are still developing. They simply don't have the neurological ability to plan how to upset you on purpose. What feels like intentional defiance is often an immature brain struggling to manage big feelings or follow instructions under stress.

<u>When we misinterpret their behavior, we end up reacting with anger instead of understanding.</u> A child who ignores cleaning their room isn't necessarily being disrespectful; they might be tired, distracted, or overwhelmed- or they simply forgot.

When you pause to think, <u>"What else could this mean?", you open the door to connection, teaching, and calm problem-solving.</u>

Today, you'll practice seeing your child's behavior through a lens of trust rather than suspicion.

## ✏️ Self-Reflection Exercise:

**What Story Did You Tell Yourself?**

Think back to a recent moment when your child did something that triggered you, like talking back, ignoring you, or rolling their eyes.

Describe one situation where your child's behavior upsets you:

_______________________________________________

_______________________________________________

What was your immediate interpretation of their behavior? (e.g., "They're being disrespectful.")

_______________________________________________

_______________________________________________

If you consider their brain development and emotions, what might have really been going on for them?

_______________________________________________

_______________________________________________

How does this new perspective change how you feel?

_______________________________________________

_______________________________________________

## 🎯 Today's Actionable Task

Today, when your child does something frustrating, pause and ask: "If their brain isn't fully developed, what might they need help with right now?"

Then, choose a calm, supportive response instead of reacting with anger.

**Example:**

**Behavior:** Your child whines and cries when asked to brush their teeth.

**Old interpretation:** "They're doing it again."

**New interpretation:** "They're struggling with transitions. Their brain finds it hard to shift activities."

**New response:** Pause, take a breath, and say, "It's hard to stop playing and go brush your brush. Do you want to brush first and I'll follow, or should we do it together?"

Write your plan:

Situation you might face today:

_______________________________________________

_______________________________________________

_______________________________________________


Old interpretation:

_______________________________________________

_______________________________________________

New interpretation:

_______________________________________________

_______________________________________________

Your calm, supportive response:

_______________________________________________

_______________________________________________

## End-of-The-Day Reflection

What did you notice about the way you interpreted your child's behavior today?

_______________________________________________

_______________________________________________

What intention do you want to carry into tomorrow to keep practicing this mindset shift?

_______________________________________________

_______________________________________________

# Day 11: My Kid Listens Only When I Yell

### Insight: Does Yelling Really Work?

Have you ever felt like yelling at your kid is your only option? Maybe you've said:

"I've asked them nicely ten times, and nothing changes until I yell."

It feels like yelling works because, in that moment, your kids finally comply.

But here's the truth:

**Yelling doesn't teach them to listen. It teaches them that you're only serious when you yell.**

Imagine you're in a meeting at work. Your manager calmly asks everyone to submit a report by Friday. A few people forget, and instead of following up respectfully, your manager storms into your office yelling, "Why haven't you submitted this yet? You're so irresponsible!" You might submit it immediately out of fear or anxiety, but next time, you'll feel resentment, stress, or dread around them. Over time, you start tuning out their calm requests because you've learned that their actual deadline comes after yelling.

Kids are the same. When calm instructions are always followed by yelling, they learn that yelling is the "real cue" to act.

This doesn't happen because your kids are bad. It happens because yelling has become a part of your communication pattern.

It's a loop:

1. You ask your child calmly.
2. They delay or ignore.
3. You repeat with frustration.
4. They continue ignoring.
5. You yell.
6. They finally respond out of fear, resentment, or just to end the yelling.

The result? They only act when your voice escalates, and your relationship fills with tension.

### ✏️ Self-Reflection Exercise:

**Your Yelling Pattern**

Think back to today or yesterday:

Describe one situation when you yelled to make your child listen.

What exactly happened?

_______________________________________________

_______________________________________________

How many times did you ask before yelling?

_______________________________________________

What was your child doing when you yelled?

_______________________________________________

_______________________________________________

How did they respond after you yelled?

_______________________________________________

_______________________________________________

How did you feel afterwards?

_______________________________________________

_______________________________________________

If you could replay that moment, what would you do differently to break the yelling cycle?

_______________________________________________

_______________________________________________

_______________________________________________

## 🎯 Today's Actionable Task

Today, practice a new approach.

When your child doesn't listen to you:

- ➤ **Pause with intention:** You might feel like shouting from across the room — but stop. Take one deep breath and tell yourself: *"I'm not yelling. I'm guiding."*
- ➤ **Get closer:** Don't give commands from a distance. Your presence matters more than your volume.
- ➤ **Connect first:** Look your child in the eye, gently touch their shoulder and make sure you have their attention. Connection calms both of you.
- ➤ **Use calm, clear words:** Say what needs to happen in a simple, direct way. No lectures, no threats - just clarity.
- ➤ **Offer 2 choices:** For example, "Do you want to brush your teeth first or put on pajamas first? Both options lead to the same goal, but they give your child a sense of control.

### 👉 Example:

- * **Situation:** Your child ignores your call to get ready for bed.
- * **Old approach:** Repeating yourself louder each time until you end up yelling.
- * **New approach:** Walk over, touch their arm gently, make eye contact, and say: "It's bedtime now. Do you want to brush your teeth first or put on pajamas first?" Then calmly follow through with the bedtime routine without yelling.

Write your plan:

A situation in which you'll practice this approach:

_______________________________________________

_______________________________________________

New calm, clear approach you'll use:

_______________________________________________

_______________________________________________

_______________________________________________

## End-of-The-Day Reflection

What happened today when you tried a calm, direct approach instead of yelling?

_______________________________________________

_______________________________________________

How did your child respond differently?

_______________________________________________

_______________________________________________

What intention do you want to carry into tomorrow to continue breaking this cycle?

_______________________________________________

_______________________________________________

# Day 12: How You Hurt Your Child

 **Insight: When Love Turns into Hurt**

No parent wakes up thinking, "I'm going to hurt my child today." But here's the uncomfortable truth:

Sometimes, in our anger, fear, or frustration, we say or do things that leave scars on our child.

Think about it:

- The moment you called them "lazy" because they didn't clean up
- When you said, "What's wrong with you?" after they spilled milk again
- When you told them, "You're just like your dad/mom," with anger in your voice

You may not even realize it, but those words often come out of your mouth like a habit. What feels like a quick reaction or common phrase to you may land very differently for your child.

What they actually hear is:

- "I'm not good enough."
- "I'm unlovable when I make mistakes."
- "I'm bad."

And here's why that matters:

Young children often struggle to distinguish between "I did something wrong" and "I am wrong."

It's a subtle difference, but it has a powerful impact on their developing sense of self. Let's say your child breaks a vase and you scold them harshly. They don't walk away thinking, "Oops, I need to be more careful next time."

They walk away thinking, "I ruin things. I make people angry. I must be bad." That's not discipline, that's shame. And shame doesn't teach. It damages. Instead, our role as parents is to correct with compassion.

Yes, we hold them accountable, but in a way that protects their dignity. You can still say:

"I know it was an accident. Let's be more careful around breakable things."

That one sentence teaches responsibility without making them feel like they are the problem.

Remember: You're not just shaping their behavior. You're shaping how they see themselves.

## ✏️ Self-Reflection Exercise: Avoid Hurtful Words

Answer honestly and without any judgment:

Are there any hurtful words or labels you find yourself saying in anger?

_______________________________________________

_______________________________________________

What do you think they felt when they heard those words?

_______________________________________________

_______________________________________________

Where do these words come from—your own upbringing, stress, fear, or frustration?

_______________________________________________

_______________________________________________

What could you say instead to guide them without shaming them?

_______________________________________________

_______________________________________________

## 🎯 Today's Actionable Task

Today, commit to not using any of the following with your child:

- ▼ Name-calling (e.g., lazy, naughty, annoying)
- ▼ Shaming statements (e.g., "What's wrong with you?")
- ▼ Comparisons (e.g., "Why can't you be like your brother?")
- ▼ Threats (e.g., "If you don't behave, no dinner tonight.")

Instead, try this:

When your child misbehaves, pause and say:

- ◆ "This behavior isn't okay, but I love you. Let's fix it together."
- ◆ "You're having a hard time right now. How can I help?"
- ◆ "It's okay to make mistakes. Let's clean this up."

Write your plan:

A phrase I will use today instead of hurtful words:

_______________________________________________

_______________________________________________


## 📊 End-of-The-Day Reflection

Did you catch yourself before using hurtful words today?

_______________________________________________


What intention will you carry into tomorrow to build them up instead of tearing them down?

_______________________________________________

_______________________________________________

# Day 13: Effects of Angry Parents on Children

## ❋ Insight: Your Child Absorbs Your Anger like a Sponge

Imagine watching your child play with their dolls or Lego figures. Suddenly, you hear them yell:

"Why can't you ever listen?! I've told you a hundred times already!"

Your stomach sinks. That voice… It's yours.

Children don't just imitate how you cook or drive. <u>They soak up your anger, your sighs, your tones, and your harsh words like a sponge</u>. And here's what many parents don't realize: <u>kids pick up our bad traits faster than our good ones.</u>

When they're young, they might throw toys or yell back. But think ahead: what will happen when they're teens? One day, they may end up using the same words, the same anger patterns, back at you. How would it feel to hear your teenager shout at you in the exact way you shout at them now?

It's sobering to realize, but it's also powerful. Because it means every time you model calm, patience, and emotional control, you're giving them lifelong tools. And every time you model yelling, shame, or harshness, you're handing those down, too.

<u>Your anger shapes their personality and how others perceive them. It becomes their inner voice. We all need to be aware of the way we handle our anger—not just for us, but for them.</u>

<u>Because to your child, **you are the world**.</u>

## ✏️ Self-Reflection Exercise:

**Your Child Mirrors You**

Have you ever seen your child get angry or speak in the same way you do using your tone, words, or reaction style?

What did you honestly feel in that moment? (e.g., guilt, sadness, surprise, discomfort, regret)

___________________________________________

___________________________________________

___________________________________________

If your child grows up using your current anger patterns with their future partner, friends, or even their own children, how would you feel?

_______________________________________________

_______________________________________________

_______________________________________________

_______________________________________________

## ⌖ Today's Actionable Task

Today, when you feel anger rising inside you, choose one of these calm statements instead of yelling or shaming:

- "That tone I just used wasn't okay. Let me try that again more calmly."
- "I can feel myself getting worked up, and I don't want to take it out on you."
- "I'm learning how to handle big feelings better, just like I want you to."

Write your plan for today:

A situation I will practice today:

_______________________________________________

_______________________________________________

_______________________________________________

Which calm phrase will I use?

_______________________________________________

_______________________________________________

## ⬛ End-of-The-Day Reflection

When you chose calm words today, what change did you notice in your child's mood or behavior?

_______________________________________________

_______________________________________________

Looking ahead, what story do you hope your child will tell themselves about love, anger, and feeling safe with you?

_______________________________________________

_______________________________________________

---

# Day 14: What Happens When You're an Angry Parent?

**✳ Insight: Your Anger Writes Their Story**

Picture this:

Your child is sitting in their room, hugging their knees, after you've yelled. They're staring at the floor, quiet. You think,

"Finally, they're listening."

But inside, they're not thinking about what they did wrong. They're thinking:

– "Why does Mom/Dad hate me?"
– "Dad/mom is scary."

Here's the truth: Kids rarely hear the lesson behind your anger. They hear the fear in your voice. They feel the sting of rejection. They begin to believe:

- "Love goes away when I'm bad."
- "People I love might hurt me when I make mistakes."
- "Big feelings are dangerous."

When anger becomes your main way of responding, it can:

○ Damage their brain development. Constant stress makes it hard for children to focus, learn, and process information clearly.

- o Hurt their emotional health. They may feel anxious, ashamed, or unworthy of love, believing they're "bad kids" instead of kids learning from mistakes.
- o Harm their social confidence. Children who are frequently exposed to anger often struggle with making new friends and expressing their feelings safely.
- o Weaken your relationship. Over time, they may pull away from you emotionally to protect themselves, making it harder for you to guide and connect with them.

But here's the hope. Your anger isn't the end of their story. Every time you choose calm words, repair after yelling, or guide them with patience, you teach them:

"Mistakes are okay. Love is safe here."

<u>Your anger is powerful. You get to choose whether it builds fear or builds safety.</u>

## ✏️ Self-Reflection Exercise:

**What Are They Learning from Your Anger?**

Today's insight showed how your anger affects your child's brain, emotions, and confidence.

Which of these impacts worries you the most right now, and why?

________________________________________

________________________________________

________________________________________

If your child believed, "I'm a bad kid" because you were angry, what would you want them to know instead?

_______________________________________________

_______________________________________________

_______________________________________________

## 🎯 Today's Actionable Task

Today, if you find yourself yelling at your child or if they look hurt or afraid because of your anger:

1. **First, calm yourself.** Remember: You can't calm your child if you're not calm yourself. Take a few deep breaths, step away for a moment if needed, and center your emotions before approaching them.

2. **Offer a sincere apology.** Kneel to their level, look into their eyes, and say:
   - "I'm sorry I yelled. That wasn't okay. You didn't deserve that."
   - "I was feeling angry, but it's my job to handle my feelings. You are not a bad kid."

**Mean what you say.** Children can feel the difference between a rushed apology to move on, and a real apology from the heart. Slow down, place a gentle hand on their shoulder or hug them if they're open to it, and let your words land with warmth.

## End-of-The-Day Reflection

Did I apologize today when I lost my temper or yelled? If so, how did I say it?

_______________________________________________

_______________________________________________

How did my child respond to my apology?

_______________________________________________

_______________________________________________

*Week 3*

# Parenting Done More Effectively

# Day 15: How to Stop Yelling at Your Child

## ❄ Insight: Calm Parenting Isn't Weak—It's Powerful

We all dream of becoming parents who don't need to yell. You may wonder:

"Will that day ever come for me?"

My answer is yes. But it doesn't happen through willpower alone. It happens when you parent with **intention**, understanding your child, and using practical skills that guide their behavior calmly and effectively.

Today, let's learn **5 powerful strategies** to stop yelling and start leading with calm authority.

### 1. Be Respectful to Your Kids

Respect doesn't mean letting kids do whatever they want. It means guiding their behavior firmly without shaming or humiliating them. Because shame doesn't teach—it wounds. Harsh words may stop a behavior in the moment, but they can leave long-term emotional scars. Speak to them the way you want them to speak to others—with calmness, clarity, and respect.

## 2. Give a Related Consequence

Consequences should teach, not punish. When a consequence is directly tied to the behavior, your child learns to connect actions with outcomes and take responsibility. When the consequence feels random or unrelated, it just feels like a lack of control or a sense of revenge.

**Example:**

If your child refuses to wear a helmet, the natural consequence is:

"No bike rides for 3 days."

That's logical and connected to the behavior.

A wrong consequence would be:

"If you don't wear your helmet, no TV for 3 days."

That doesn't teach safety, it just adds to frustration.

**Think:** <u>Does this consequence teach the right lesson?</u> If it does, you're parenting with purpose, not punishment.

## 3. Consistent Follow Through

<u>If you say it, mean it.</u> Kids learn quickly whether you keep your word. Following through every time—calmly, not angrily—builds trust and respect for your boundaries.

**Example:**

If they ignore homework, they'll need to finish it during their playtime before doing anything else fun. You don't have to raise your voice—you just have to follow through.

### 4. Set Expectations Clearly

Before entering any situation, clearly communicate to your child what you expect. Tell them clearly, before the problem happens. Setting expectations ahead of time helps prevent frustration and power struggles.

**Example:**

"At the store, we're buying only groceries today. No candy."

Clear expectations reduce surprises and resistance.

### 5. Ask Your Child to Repeat the Rule

After giving an instruction or boundary, ask your child to repeat it back to you. This helps them process what you said and gives you a chance to clarify misunderstandings before conflict starts.

**Example:**

"Can you tell me what we're doing at the store today?"

When they say it back, they're more likely to remember and follow through.

## ✏️ Self-Reflection Exercise:

**Apply the 5 Steps for Calm Authority**

Which of the 5 steps do you feel most confident using right now? Why does that one feel easier for you??

_______________________________________________

_______________________________________________

_______________________________________________

Which step do you find the hardest to put into action? Why?

_______________________________________________

_______________________________________________

_______________________________________________

How might your parenting feel different if you practice all 5 steps consistently?

_______________________________________________

_______________________________________________

_______________________________________________

## 🎯 Today's Actionable Task

Choose one common stress trigger (like toothbrushing, bedtime stalling, or ignoring instructions). Now, mentally walk through how you would respond using all five calm authority steps. Ask yourself:

How will I speak to my child? (Will I stay calm and respectful, even if I'm frustrated?)

___________________________________________

___________________________________________

What is a related consequence I can give, if needed? (Is it directly connected to the behavior?)

___________________________________________

___________________________________________

Will I follow through consistently? (Or do I give in sometimes and lose credibility?)

___________________________________________

___________________________________________

Am I setting clear expectations in advance? (Did I tell them what I expect before the conflict starts?)

___________________________________________

___________________________________________

Can I ask them to repeat what they heard? (Do they understand the rule or boundary?)

_______________________________________

_______________________________________

## End-of-The-Day Reflection

How did practicing this strategy change your child's response?

_______________________________________

_______________________________________

_______________________________________

How did it feel for you to parent calmly and with clear boundaries?

_______________________________________

_______________________________________

# Day 16: Simple No-Yelling Checklist

### ❈ Insight: Why Yelling Feels Easier but Isn't Effective

We all want to be those parents who don't need to yell. But yelling often becomes our automatic reaction when we're stressed or triggered.

The truth is: Yelling feels easy and powerful, but it rarely works long-term. It teaches kids to obey out of fear, not understanding. Today, instead of aiming for perfection, let's focus on three simple but powerful shifts you can make to break the yelling habit.

- 1. Check Your Language

Your words carry weight, and kids carry those words in their hearts.

We often don't realize how deeply our everyday words shape our children. One parent shared how a single phrase from *their own parent* - "Why can't you ever do anything right?" - left a lasting scar. Even now, they battle self-doubt in nearly everything they do. If blaming, criticizing, or shaming is your default response, that's what will come out when you're angry.

You must check your language.

Are you attacking the behavior or the child? Kids can only grow if they feel safe in your words.

> ➢ Instead of: "You're so annoying!"
>   ☑ Try: "That behavior is annoying me right now."

> ➢ Instead of: "I'm ashamed of you."
>   ☑ Try: "I'm not okay with that behavior."

When you separate the behavior from your child's identity, they can actually hear you without feeling worthless.

- 2. Check Your Thoughts and Behavior

What we believe shapes how we react.

If you think, "They're doing this on purpose to make me mad," you'll explode faster. But what if the behavior is actually a call for help, and not a personal attack?

Pause and ask:
- "What's really triggering me here?"
- "What am I feeling right now, and why?"

When you shift from blame to curiosity, you gain emotional control and a perspective.

- 3. Check Your Self-Regulation

Before you try to correct your child, check yourself first.

Ask:

- "Am I calm enough to handle this wisely?"
- "Is this coming from my own emotions, or am I truly trying to help my child grow?"

If your heart is racing, your voice is rising, or your body feels tense, pause, breathe, and reset. <u>Your child is not your emotional trash can.</u>

<u>The way you express anger becomes the way they internalize emotion.</u>

<u>Your words plant seeds in your child's heart and brain</u>—make sure they're seeds you want to grow.

Self-regulation isn't about ignoring problems. It's about leading with clarity and compassion—the kind your child learns to mirror.

## ✎ Self-Reflection Exercise: Check Yourself

Which step do you feel you need to focus on the most right now, and why? (Think about your recent parenting moments—what keeps showing up?)?

_______________________________________________

_______________________________________________

_______________________________________________

_______________________________________________

## 🎯 Today's Actionable Task

Think back to a tough moment with your child today (or recently).

Choose one step from today's checklist that felt uncomfortable and write how you would handle that moment differently next time.

______________________________________________

______________________________________________

______________________________________________

______________________________________________

## 📊 End-of-The-Day Reflection

What difference did it make today when you used the checklist before reacting?

______________________________________________

______________________________________________

______________________________________________

# Day 17: Parenting Methods That Don't Work

### ✳ Insight: Why Don't Yelling & Spanking Work?

Today, many parents are aware—thanks to books, media, and parenting education—that yelling and physical punishment are ineffective. But in the heat of the moment, we often react the way we were raised. Without even realizing it, our hand might reach for a child's arm, or our voice might rise because that's what was modeled to us growing up.

You might even catch yourself thinking, "A light smack on the hand or back isn't harmful," or "Some kids need a little spanking to learn." But here's the truth: yelling and spanking might get short-term obedience, but they don't teach self-control- they teach fear. They don't guide your child's heart. They just shut your child down.

Let's be honest—no parent is always calm and smiling. That's unrealistic. But what we can build is a steady, respectful parenting framework we return to, especially when things get hard.

So, if you feel your hand rising in frustration, pause, intentionally.

Without intention, we naturally drift toward what's familiar- raising our voice, yelling, reacting with anger. But intention creates a new path: lower your voice with calm authority. Instead of pulling away, reach out with connection. Look your child in the eyes and calmly say what needs to be done next.

Yes, this kind of parenting takes intention, not perfection.

But every time you choose a connection over control, you break an old cycle and build something better.

## ✐ Self-Reflection Exercise: Learn from the Past

Growing up, were you raised under yelling or spanking?

_________________________________________________

How did it make you feel as a child?

_________________________________________________

_________________________________________________

_________________________________________________

Do you still believe spanking is necessary for raising your kids? Why or why not?

_________________________________________________

_________________________________________________

_________________________________________________

## 🎯 Today's Actionable Task

Today, when your child misbehaves, choose NOT to yell or use any physical punishment. Instead:

______________________________________________________________

______________________________________________________________

Write your plan here: What will I say or do instead of yelling or spanking?

______________________________________________________________

______________________________________________________________

______________________________________________________________

## 📗 End-of-The-Day Reflection

How did it feel to respond without yelling or spanking today?

______________________________________________________________

______________________________________________________________

What do you want to remember about this experience for tomorrow?

______________________________________________________________

______________________________________________________________

# Day 18: Parenting Methods That Work

## ❉ Insight: Why Conscious Parenting?

Why do we keep repeating the same yelling or punishment patterns even though we know they don't work? Because most of our parenting happens on autopilot—we react from habit, stress, or old wounds rather than intention.

Conscious parenting changes this.

It's not about being a perfect, calm parent. <u>It's about becoming aware of your triggers, beliefs, and childhood patterns so you can respond to your children with clarity instead of reacting emotionally</u>.

Many parents think, "Why should I change when it's my child who's misbehaving?" But here's the truth: when you parent unconsciously, you're parenting from your past. You're simply repeating what you learned growing up, even if you promised yourself you wouldn't.

Conscious parenting invites you to pause and ask:

- ✓ Why am I feeling so angry right now?
- ✓ What does my child actually need in this moment?

<u>It means shifting from "How do I control my child?" to "How do I lead and guide them with awareness and love?"</u>

When you choose conscious parenting, you're not just managing your child's behavior; <u>you're teaching them how to manage themselves by modeling calmness, awareness, and emotional responsibility</u>.

This is how you break generational cycles and raise children who feel safe, respected, and deeply connected to you, even on the hard days.

## ✏️ Self-Reflection Exercise: Check Before You Act

Take a moment to reflect honestly:

When was the last time I reacted on autopilot rather than with intention? What happened?

______________________________________________

______________________________________________

______________________________________________

What is one trigger from my childhood that influences how I react to my child today?

______________________________________________

______________________________________________

______________________________________________

How would parenting feel different if I paused to understand my child before reacting?

------

------

------

## 🎯 Today's Actionable Task

Think of a moment today (or recently) when you lost your temper with your child. Using conscious parenting (awareness), ask yourself:

**"What could I have done differently if I had paused and responded with intention?"**

Write your reflection here:

------

------

------

## 🏛 End-of-The-Day Reflection

Did I catch myself parenting on autopilot today? What did I notice?

------

------

What intention do I want to carry into tomorrow to keep growing as a conscious parent?

------

------

# Day 19: How to Keep Your Cool When Kids Push Your Buttons?

### ❄ Insight: You Can't Control Your Child, But You Can Control Your Response

Kids push limits—not because they're trying to push your buttons, but because their brains literally aren't capable of thinking about your buttons.

They're not trying to make your life hard. They're just having a hard time processing their emotions. They whine, stall, yell, ignore you- all before 8 a.m.- and you might start thinking,

"They're doing this on purpose." But they're not being manipulative, they're just being developmentally appropriate.

A young brain is wired for impulse, not reflection. They're not thinking, "Let me drive Mom crazy today." They're thinking, "I don't want to stop playing," or "This feels unfair."

Still, it's easy to lose it. When your child becomes upset or refuses, your nervous system responds. You feel disrespected. Triggered. Powerless.

🔁 Try This Instead: The **R.E.S**. Technique

When you feel yourself pushed past your limit, use this 3-step reset:

1. **Recognize** what's happening. Say it out loud if needed: "I feel really overwhelmed right now."
2. **Exhale**—release a slow, long breath out. This helps your brain shift out of survival mode faster than just "deep breathing."
3. **Shift** your response with intention:

Use a calm, clear phrase: "You can do it yourself, or I'll help you."

"We'll talk about this when we're both calm."

## ✏️ Self-Reflection Exercise: Respond Wisely

What is one of your most vulnerable buttons that you find yourself reacting to the most?

_______________________________________________

_______________________________________________

How did you respond today when that button was pushed? Did you yell, shut down, stay calm, or something else?

_______________________________________________

_______________________________________________

## ◎ Today's Actionable Task

Pick one moment today when your buttons were pushed.

Now practice this reset in real life:

Notice what triggered you.

_______________________________________________

_______________________________________________

Pause and name how you feel.

_______________________________________________

_______________________________________________

Choose a calmer response on purpose.

_______________________________________

_______________________________________

_______________________________________


## End-of-The-Day Reflection

"I used to believe that my child was making my life harder on purpose. But today I learned that kids don't have the brain capacity to push my buttons intentionally—they're just having a hard time."

Next time my buttons are pushed, how can I remind myself of this truth and respond differently?

_______________________________________

_______________________________________

_______________________________________

# Day 20: Effective Tips for Staying Cool Emotionally

**✳ Insight: Staying Cool is a Choice, not a Personality Trait**

Have you ever thought:

- "I wish I didn't lose it so fast."
- "I try to stay calm, but it just happens before I know it."

Here's the truth: **Calm isn't a personality trait. It's a skill.**

No one is born knowing how to stay calm when a child screams "NO!" for the tenth time. Staying cool is a **practical choice** you build through awareness and practice, not something only "patient people" can do.

When you choose to pause before reacting, you're actually rewiring your brain to respond with **intention instead of instinct.** Today, let's explore 3 simple but powerful tools to help you stay calm in real parenting moments, not just in theory.

## 🔧 **3 Real Tools** to Stay Cool in the Heat of the Moment

- **1. Step Back, Say Less**

When you feel that you are about to explode, <u>stop talking and step back.</u> Even one step can interrupt the explosion.

Say in your head: "I can't teach right now. I need to calm down first."

This protects the moment from becoming something you'll regret.

- **2. Anchor Your Body**

Your nervous system needs a physical signal to stop the spiral.

Try one of these grounding actions:

- Press your hand to your chest and breathe into it
- Grip a cold surface (fridge handle, countertop)
- Clench and release your fists behind your back

These micro-actions help your brain shift out of fight-or-flight—even before you say a word.

- **3. Have a Go-To Reset Phrase**

When your child is melting down, you need a phrase that anchors you.

Try one of the following or create your own:

- "This isn't personal."
- "Their storm isn't my storm."
- "I'm the safe place. I don't add more chaos."

Say it quietly to yourself like a mantra. Over time, it rewires your brain to stay steady when your buttons get pushed.

## ✏️ Self-Reflection Exercise: Steps for Staying Cool

Of the 3 tips from today, which one do you think would actually help you the most when required?

___________________________________________

___________________________________________

Do you have a personal go-to strategy that helps you calm down when you feel angry? What is it?

___________________________________________

___________________________________________

___________________________________________

## ◎ Today's Actionable Task

Choose one moment today when you feel frustration rising. Instead of reacting, pause and use one of the 3 tools from today.

When I start to feel angry or overwhelmed, I will try this tool:

☐ Step back and say nothing

☐ Anchor my body (e.g., hand to chest, cold surface)

☐ Use a reset phrase (e.g., "This isn't personal.")

Write your reset phrase here:

______________________________________________

______________________________________________

______________________________________________


## 📑 End-of-The-Day Reflection

What is one intention you want to carry into tomorrow to keep building this skill?

______________________________________________

______________________________________________

______________________________________________

# Day 21: Anger Strategies for Everyday Problems

**✻ Insight: It's Not Just About Fixing Behavior- It's About Teaching Skills**

Morning routines turn into chaos when they refuse to get dressed. Homework time becomes a battle of wills. Dinner is filled with complaints about food. Bedtime drags on forever with endless requests for water, hugs, and one more story.

By the end of the day, your patience is gone. You lie in bed replaying every shout, every sigh, every moment you lose your cool and you wonder:

"How can I get through to them without yelling all day?"
"Why is parenting so exhausting?"

Here's a powerful truth:

Most parenting struggles aren't personal attacks. They're simply your kids showing you what skills they haven't yet mastered. Skills like emotional regulation, problem-solving, communication, and self-control.

Today, let's look at practical ways to respond to anger triggers, not with frustration, but with the mindset of a teacher. Because when you teach instead of reacting, you don't just solve today's problem; you build your child's confidence for life.

## 🔑 Real-Life Strategies for Everyday Problems

These everyday challenges - backtalk, lying, dawdling, and mealtime battles aren't just "bad behaviors." These are signs that your child is still developing emotional regulation, problem-solving skills, and learning how to feel safe while expressing themselves.

### -   1. Backtalk

**<u>Why it happens:</u>** Kids backtalk when they feel powerless or ignored. It's their clumsy way of saying, "See me!"

**<u>What to do:</u>** Stay calm. Say, "I hear you're upset, but that was rude. Try again with kinder words."

**<u>Why it works:</u>** They learn that feelings are okay, but rude words aren't the way to express them.

- ## 2. Lying

**Why it happens:** Most lies come from fear of getting in trouble or disappointing you.

**Example:**

A child might say, "He hit me first!" even if they started it. Why? Because the part where *they* got hurt feels bigger in their memory.

**What to do:** Instead of scolding, say, "Thanks for being honest. Let's figure out how to fix this together."

**Why it works:** When kids feel safe, they tell the truth more often.

- ## 3. Dawdling/Not Listening

**Why it happens:** Kids stall when they feel rushed or disconnected. Moving slowly is their silent protest.

**What to do:** Break tasks into small steps. Add playful urgency: "First socks, then shoes. Let's see if you can beat my count to ten!"

**Why it works:** You turn stress into connection, and kids move faster when they feel seen.

- ## 4. Mealtime Tantrums

**Why it happens:** Saying "no" to food gives kids a feeling of control. It's not always about the food.

**What to do:** Don't overthink it as "my child is spoiled" or "I'm failing as a parent." Just stay calm and offer simple choices. For example: "You don't have to eat broccoli. Do you want carrot or cucumber instead?"

**Why it works:** They feel respected, and that lowers the power struggle.

 **Remember:**

These behaviors are frustrating, but they're normal. Your calm response is one of the most powerful tools you have.

## ✎ Self-Reflection Exercise: Check Your Triggers

Which of these everyday problems triggers your anger the fastest? (Check all that apply.)

☐ Backtalk

☐ Lying

☐ Dawdling

☐ Mealtime tantrums

☐ Other: _______________________________

Why do you think this behavior bothers you so much? (e.g., feels disrespectful, makes me late, triggers my childhood memories)

## 🎯 Today's Actionable Task

Choose one problematic behavior today.

When it happens:

Pause and remind yourself: "They're not trying to make my life hard. They're showing me what they still need to learn." Use the teaching strategy from today's insight instead of reacting with anger.

📝 Write down which one you will practice:

What misbehavior will you focus on today?

_______________________________________________

_______________________________________________

_______________________________________________

What strategy will you try instead of reacting with anger?

_______________________________________________

_______________________________________________

_______________________________________________

## 📋 End-of-The-Day Reflection

What small shift do I want to continue practicing tomorrow?

_______________________________________________

_______________________________________________

_______________________________________________

# Week 4

## No More
## Angry Parent

# Day 22: The Weight of Parent Guilt

**Insight: Why Do We Carry Parent Guilt and Why Does It Matter**

This topic isn't directly from the book *Angry Parent, Angry Child*, but it's an essential piece for becoming a calmer, more intentional parent.

Have you ever thought,

- "If only I had been more patient today…"
- "I shouldn't have yelled at them like that…"
- "I should have played with them more…"
- "Why am I like this?"

Even good parents feel guilt sometimes, especially good parents. Because you care so deeply, your mind fills with endless "what ifs":

- What if I'm messing them up forever?
- What if they grow up feeling unloved?
- What if I'm not doing enough?

Working parents often feel guilty for not spending enough time with their kids. To ease that guilt, they might buy expensive toys or allow extra screen time as compensation. But here's the hard truth:

**Guilt doesn't make you a better parent. It makes you a more exhausted, anxious parent.**

Your child doesn't need a perfect parent who sacrifices everything out of guilt. They need a parent who is calm, present, and willing to keep learning. Guilt focuses on *"I'm bad,"* while reflection focuses on *"What can I do differently next time?"*

**Remember:** Feeling guilty shows that you care. Using that guilt to reflect, grow, and change is what makes you a better parent.

## ✎ Self-Reflection Exercise: Your Parenting Guilt

Write honestly:

What are the top 3 things you feel guilty about in your parenting right now?

_______________________________________________

_______________________________________________

_______________________________________________

Where do you think this guilt comes from? (Your childhood, social media comparisons, fear of judgment, unrealistic expectations)

_______________________________________________

_______________________________________________

When you feel guilty, how does it affect the way you interact with your child?

_______________________________________________

_______________________________________________

## ◎ Today's Actionable Task

Practice this guilt-to-growth reframing exercise today:

When you notice any guilt rising (e.g., "I yelled again today"), pause and say: *"I feel guilty because I care. What can I learn from this moment?"* Write your reframed thought here:

Guilty thought:

_______________________________________________

_______________________________________________

_______________________________________________

Growth reflection:

_______________________________________________

_______________________________________________

_______________________________________________

Choose one small action to do differently next time.

_______________________________________________

_______________________________________________

_______________________________________________

## ⬛ End-of-The-Day Reflection

What was the heaviest guilt you felt today?

_______________________________________________

_______________________________________________

_______________________________________________

How did it feel to replace guilt with learning and intention?

_______________________________________________

_______________________________________________

_______________________________________________

# Day 23: What is Self-Care?

## ✳ Insight: Why Does Self-Care Matter?

Have you ever noticed how easy it is to snap at your kids when your own energy is down?

Think about it. You wake up tired because you have stayed up late cleaning or finishing work. You skip breakfast because you're busy packing lunchboxes. You don't even have a moment to sit and breathe before the demands start:

- ✓ "Mom, where's my uniform?"
- ✓ "Dad, I don't want that for breakfast!"
- ✓ "Can you help me with my project right now?"

It's no wonder you feel like exploding before 8 am.

When we don't care for ourselves, our bodies and minds go into survival mode. Little things feel big. We react instead of responding.

It's like running a car with no fuel; eventually, it will stop in the middle of the road, no matter how desperately you need to keep going.

Many parents think self-care is selfish or luxurious, like spa days or expensive trips. But true self-care isn't about indulgence; it's about maintenance. Just like charging your phone, self-care recharges you, so you don't burn out and take your exhaustion out on your kids.

Here's the truth: The less you care for yourself, the more easily anger takes over.

When you're well-rested, nourished, and calm, you can think clearly. You can parent intentionally. You can set healthy boundaries with love rather than shouting out of overwhelm.

Self-care isn't about becoming a "perfect parent." It's about becoming a present parent, the kind your kids need—the one who can pause before reacting, listen before lecturing, and hold space for their child's big feelings without being drowned by your own.

## ✎ Self-Reflection Exercise: Fill Your Cup First

Answer honestly:

How do I usually feel when I'm running low on sleep or rest?

______________________________________

______________________________________

When I'm tired, how do I react to my kids' normal misbehaviors?

________________________________________

________________________________________

What's one thing I've stopped doing for myself because I'm "too busy"?

________________________________________

________________________________________

How can self-care help me manage my anger better?

________________________________________

________________________________________

## ◎ Today's Actionable Task

Write down 3 simple self-care actions you can take today that don't require extra money or much time.

**Example:**

- ➢ Drink a full glass of water before your morning coffee
- ➢ Step outside for 3 minutes of fresh air alone
- ➢ Go to bed 15 minutes earlier than usual tonight

________________________________________

________________________________________

________________________________________

Choose one and do it today.



## End-of-The-Day Reflection

Did I notice any difference in my mood or reactions when I took care of myself today?

________________________________________

________________________________________

What do I want to keep doing tomorrow to recharge myself?

________________________________________

________________________________________

# Day 24: The Best Self-Care Checklist

### ❋ Insight: Why Does This Checklist Matter?

Yesterday, we explored what self-care really means, not bubble baths or expensive treats, but **taking care of your basic needs** to be a calmer, more present parent. Today, let's dig deeper into the **practical self-care checkpoints** discussed in the book *Angry Parent, Angry Child*.

The book reminds us that **self-care isn't optional**. Just like we check if our kids have eaten, slept, and moved their bodies, we need to check ourselves, too. Because when we ignore ourselves, anger and frustration show up uninvited.

Think about it:

- Have you ever yelled at your child simply because you were exhausted?
- Have you ever snapped because you haven't eaten properly all day?
- Have you felt overwhelmed because you were trying to do everything at once?

We're not robots. Today's checklist will help you **pause and reflect on your sleep, movement, and multitasking habits.** Without these, even the best parenting strategies can't work effectively.

# ✏️ Self-Reflection Exercise: Take Care of Yourself

## 1. Are You Getting Enough Sleep?

Many parents act like sleep isn't a big deal, but it really is. Sleep is how your body and mind recharge. When you don't get enough sleep, you're more likely to feel overwhelmed, snap at your kids, and struggle to stay calm.

Your body and brain are connected. If your body is tired, your mind will be, too. Sleep helps you stay patient, think clearly, and respond thoughtfully instead of reacting impulsively. Getting rest isn't selfish, it's one of the best things you can do for your child.

**Answer the following Questions:**

What time do you normally go to bed? _______________________

How many hours of sleep do you need to feel your best? __________

What small change can you make to sleep better tonight?

_______________________________________________________

_______________________________________________________

## 2. Are You Exercising?

Exercise isn't about going to the gym. Even a short walk, yoga stretch, or dancing with your kids **can reduce stress hormones, increase energy, and uplift mood**. With movement, your body stores stress, making anger more explosive.

**Answer the following Questions:**

How important do you think movement or exercise is for your parenting?

---

---

How often do you move your body during the day?

---

Is there a small way you could fit in 10–20 minutes of movement today?

---

## 3. Are You a Multitasker?

Multitasking might feel productive, especially in parenting, but it actually drains your energy because your brain is constantly switching. Over time, it can leave you burned out, impatient, and overwhelmed. And your kids can sense when you're only half-present.

**Answer the following Questions:**

What are the tasks you usually multitask that truly matter, and which ones don't?

---

---

Is there anything you can remove or simplify instead of multitasking?

---

---

## ◎ Today's Actionable Task

Choose one area (sleep, exercise, or multitasking) to focus on improving today.

What will I do differently today to take care of myself better?

______________________________________

______________________________________

______________________________________


## ▦ End-of-The-Day Reflection

How did taking care of yourself today affect your mood, energy, or parenting?

______________________________________

______________________________________

# Day 25: Working as a Team

### ✻ Insight: When Parents Aren't Aligned, Kids Get Confused

Have you ever felt like you're doing it all alone—dishes, laundry, grocery shopping, bedtime routines—while feeling resentful that your partner doesn't notice how hard you're working?

Or maybe you've heard these conversations before:

- **Wife:** "You're never here. You hardly help at all."
- **Husband:** "You never appreciate what I do here."

These words aren't just about chores. They're cries for teamwork.

Parenting should not be a solo mission. When you try to handle everything yourself, you end up exhausted, snappy, and disconnected from both your kids and partner.

Your anger often isn't about your child's spilled cereal or homework complaints; it's about carrying the invisible weight of everything alone.

Here's the truth:

When parents aren't aligned, kids get confused. When you and your partner argue, criticize each other in front of your kids, or give mixed messages (one says yes, one says no), it creates insecurity.

Kids quickly figure out which parent will give in and which to avoid. Your calm boundaries lose power when they're not backed up as a team.

Being a good teammate doesn't mean you always agree.

It means:

- Backing each other up in front of the kids (even if you disagree later in private).
- Sharing responsibilities instead of expecting your partner to read your mind.
- Communicating your needs instead of letting silent resentment build up.

When you and your partner work together, kids feel safer, your anger reduces, and your home feels calmer.

## ✏ Self-Reflection Exercise:

### How Well Do You and Your Partner Work as a Parenting Team?

Reflect honestly on your current teamwork in parenting. What patterns do you notice? (Check that applies)

1. When a parenting decision needs to be made, do you usually

    ☐ Discuss it ahead of time

    ☐ Wing it in the moment

    ☐ One parent decides without the other

2. When your child acts up, do you and your partner

    ☐ Support each other (even if you discuss it later)

    ☐ Disagree openly in front of the child

    ☐ One parent steps in while the other pulls back

3. Do you find yourself thinking:

    ☐ "I wish they helped out more."

    ☐ "They never appreciate what I do."

    ☐ "I don't even want to ask because it ends up in a fight."

## 🎯 Today's Actionable Task

Based on what you noticed from the self-reflection questions, what did you realize about how you and your partner work together?

Write down a thought or small step you'll try to communicate better today:

_______________________________________________

_______________________________________________

_______________________________________________

_______________________________________________

## 📋 End-of-The-Day Reflection

What happened when you asked for support from your partner today?

_______________________________________________

_______________________________________________

_______________________________________________

What is one thing you appreciate about your partner's efforts today?

_______________________________________________

_______________________________________________

_______________________________________________

# Day 26: Less Angry Parenting Routine

## 🌸 Insight: The Secret Calm Button for Parents

Have you ever noticed how your mornings feel like a mini battlefield?

One kid is still half-asleep under the blanket, another is crying because their cereal bowl isn't the blue one, and you're yelling from the kitchen, *"Hurry up or we're going to be late!"* By the time you get everyone out the door, your anger has already drained half your energy for the rest of the day.

And then bedtime comes. You're exhausted, your child is stalling— *"One more drink of water… one more story…"* and before you know it, you're snapping at them to sleep, feeling guilty as you close their door.

Here's a secret many calm parents know:

Routines are like invisible calm buttons.

Think about it. When you walk into your favorite coffee shop, you know exactly what to order and how it'll taste. That predictability feels comforting, right? Kids are the same. Morning and bedtime routines create predictability, and predictability creates safety for them and you.

**Morning routines** aren't about being a super-organized Pinterest parent. It's simply waking up 10 minutes earlier so you can sip your coffee in peace or setting out tomorrow's clothes the night before so there's one less meltdown about the dinosaur shirt being in the laundry.

**Bedtime routines** aren't about elaborate skincare rituals and herbal tea (though that sounds nice too). It's about dimming the lights, reading one short story, brushing teeth without a wrestling match, and ending the day with "I love you, see you in the morning."

**How does this matter for anger?**

When your brain knows what's coming next, it doesn't go into panic mode. The calmer you feel, the less likely you'll explode over small things, like spilled juice or toothpaste blobs on the mirror.

Routines won't turn you into a perfect parent overnight. But they will make you a calmer one. Calmer parents raise kids who feel safe, loved, and ready to face the world confidently.

Today, let's build routines that act like little anchors in your day, keeping you steady no matter how wild the parenting waves get.

## ✏️ Self-Reflection Exercise: Set Your Routines Straight

### 🟦 Morning Routine:

What does your typical morning look like?

_______________________________________________

_______________________________________________

What part of your morning makes you the most stressed or rushed?

_______________________________________________

_______________________________________________

What is one small change you can make to feel calmer in the morning?

_______________________________________________

_______________________________________________

### 🌙 Bedtime Routine:

How does bedtime usually go in your home?

_______________________________________________

_______________________________________________

What part of bedtime triggers frustration or impatience in you?

_______________________________________________

_______________________________________________

What is one small calming step you can add to your bedtime routine tonight?

_______________________________________________

_______________________________________________

## 🎯 Today's Actionable Task

Create Your Calm Routine List

Write down:

2 small changes for tomorrow's morning routine (e.g., wake up 10 mins earlier, lay out clothes before going to bed).

_______________________________________________

_______________________________________________

_______________________________________________

A small change for tonight's bedtime routine (e.g., Dim lights after dinner, read a short calming story before sleep).

_______________________________________________

_______________________________________________

_______________________________________________

Post it somewhere you can see—such as a bathroom mirror, fridge, or next to your bed. Remind yourself: "I am creating calm for myself and my kids."

## ▚ End-of-The-Day Reflection

How did your child respond to your calmer approach this morning or evening?

______________________________________________

______________________________________________

______________________________________________

What will you continue tomorrow to build these calm habits into your daily parenting life?

______________________________________________

______________________________________________

# Day 27: Parenting Mindset Reset

### ✳ Insight: Your Mindset Shapes Your Parenting

There are days when parenting feels heavier than it should. You wake up already feeling tense, thinking, "I have to get them ready. I have to deal with their whining. I have to cook, clean, drive…"

But here's a truth that many parents overlook:

The way you think about your child and your parenting role shapes how you feel and act. When you think, "My child is so difficult," every request, spill, or refusal feels like an attack. You react with irritation and anger.

But when you think, "They're just a child, learning their way," you soften. You pause before responding. You remember they're growing, not trying to make your day harder.

## Have To vs. Get To

Most parents think in "have to":

- "I have to feed them breakfast."
- "I have to drive them to school."
- "I have to deal with their tantrum."

But what if you shift to "get to":

- "I get to nourish them with breakfast today."
- "I get to hear their little stories on the way to school."

- "I get to guide them through big feelings."

**"Have to" feels like an obligation. "Get to" feels like a privilege.**

This isn't just fluffy positive thinking. It changes everything. "Have to" feels heavy and builds resentment. "Get to" feels like an opportunity to love and serve.

When you believe, "This is just a tough moment, we'll get through it," you stay calm and solution-focused. When you believe, "My child is impossible; nothing works," you spiral into frustration and anger.

Your child senses your mindset. If they feel seen as "the difficult one," they live up to that label. If they feel seen as a child who is learning and growing, they rise to meet it.

## ✏️ Self-Reflection Exercise: Mindset Reset Practice

Think of a moment this week when you felt parenting was a burden.

What was your thought at that moment?

________________________________________

________________________________________

________________________________________

Rewrite that thought by shifting from "have to" to "get to."

________________________________________

________________________________________

________________________________________

**Example:**

**Original:** "I have to clean up their mess again."

**Shifted:** "I get to create a clean, safe space for them to play and learn."

## Today's Actionable Task

Think of something you usually say or feel like you "have to" do that feels heavy or stressful.

Write it down below. Then try shifting it into a "get to" - a way to see it with more purpose, meaning, or even gratitude.

**Example:**

"I have to get them ready for bed." → "I get to help them end their day feeling loved and calm."

What's one "have to" task that feels heavy for you?

___________________________________________________

___________________________________________________

How could you rewrite it as a "get to" today?

___________________________________________________

___________________________________________________

## End-of-The-Day Reflection

Did shifting from "have to" to "get to" change how you felt today?

___________________________________________________

___________________________________________________

___________________________________________________

# Day 28: Letter to Yourself

**✳ Insight: Honoring Your Journey—From Surviving to Loving**

Today marks the end of your 4-week journey. Pause for a moment. Breathe deeply.

You started this workbook because you wanted change. Because you were tired of feeling angry, tired of yelling, tired of the guilt that followed. And here you are—28 days later—having shown up, reflected, and chosen growth every single day.

Parenting isn't easy. Some days feel heavy, with endless responsibilities, tantrums, and worries. But as you've learned, the way you see your role changes everything.

When you think, "I have to do this," life feels like an obligation. But when you think, "I get to do this," you realize parenting is a privilege. You get to watch your child grow. You get to hold them when they cry. You get to guide them towards who they're meant to become.

This isn't about perfection. It's about choosing connection over control. Presence over performance. Love over fear.

Today, as you close this chapter, write a letter to yourself. Let it be your reminder of who you're becoming and how far you've come.

## ✏️ Self-Reflection Exercise: Letter to Yourself

Reflect on these before writing your letter:

What have I learned about myself in these 4 weeks?

_______________________________________________

_______________________________________________

_______________________________________________

What did I learn about my triggers and anger patterns?

_______________________________________________

_______________________________________________

_______________________________________________

What did I learn about my child's needs and behaviors?

_______________________________________________

_______________________________________________

_______________________________________________

What kind of parent do I truly want to be?

_______________________________________________

_______________________________________________

_______________________________________________

##  Today's Actionable Task

Before you close this workbook, take one more moment—just for you.

You've done something deeply meaningful these past 28 days. Not just for your child, but for yourself. And that deserves to be honored.

So today, write a letter from your heart. Not to your child. Not to anyone else. But to you.

Speak with kindness. Speak honestly. Speak like someone who's learned, struggled, grown, and still hopes.

In your letter, you might:

- Celebrate your strength for showing up through the hard days
- Acknowledge the moments you wanted to give up but didn't
- Remember what kind of parent you want to be
- Offer yourself love, hope, and grace to keep going

Start your letter:

**Dear Me,**

I am proud of you because…

I've learned that parenting is…

I want to remember that…

My hope for myself and my child is…

Dear Me,

Dear Me,

 "Parenting is like planting a seed—you may not see the growth every day, but with patience, love, and care, you are nurturing roots that will one day grow strong and bear fruit."

# Conclusion

**🫶 You've reached the end of this 4-week journey.**

Take a moment to pause and breathe. Let yourself feel the weight of what you've just accomplished.

Over these past weeks, you've looked honestly at yourself, your anger, your guilt, your triggers, your tears behind closed doors. You've faced parts of yourself that felt heavy to carry. That alone is something most people never find the courage to do.

You've chosen to try again, to understand your child's heart a little deeper, and to soften yours along the way. Some days, you probably felt like nothing was working. Some days, it felt easier to slip back into old habits. But still, here you are, reading these words- a quiet but powerful sign that you care deeply enough to keep going.

I want you to know: You are not the same parent you were a month ago.

You may still yell sometimes. You may still feel your patience run out. That doesn't mean you've failed. It means you're human. Parenting isn't about perfection. It's about repair. It's about apologizing after you snap. It's about sitting beside your child after the meltdown and saying, "That was hard for both of us, wasn't it?" It's about loving them through their hardest days and loving yourself through yours.

If you take nothing else away from this book, please remember this:

**You are exactly the parent your child needs right now.**

Not because you're calmer, smarter, or more "put together." But because you're you—willing to keep learning, keep trying, and keep loving.

As you close this book, I hope you carry these truths with you:

Your child isn't here to make your life hard. They're here to grow alongside you.

You don't have to do this alone.

Every moment is a chance to choose to love again.

Thank you for letting me walk these 28 days with you. It has been an honor to sit with your pain, your hope, and your love.

Here's to your next breath, your next hug, your next whispered apology, your next belly laugh. That is where parenting lives. And that is where your child will always find you.

With love, grace, and so much hope for you,

*Carrie Khang*

# References


Siegel, D. J., & Bryson, T. P. (2011). *The Whole-Brainchild: 12 Revolutionary Strategies to Nurture Your Child's Developing Mind.* New York, NY: Delacorte Press. Cited for: Brain development, prefrontal cortex immaturity, dysregulation, emotion coaching.

Brown, B. (2012). *Daring Greatly: How the Courage to Be Vulnerable Transforms the Way We Live, Love, Parent, and Lead.* New York, NY: Gotham Books. Cited for: Effects of shame, vulnerability, parenting with empathy.

Nelsen, J., Lott, L., & Glenn, S. (2006). *Positive Discipline.* New York, NY: Ballantine Books. Cited for: Discipline vs. punishment, long-term effectiveness of parenting tools.

Faber, A., & Mazlish, E. (2012). *How to Talk So Kids Will Listen & Listen So Kids Will Talk.* New York, NY: Scribner. Cited for: Respectful communication, emotional validation, alternatives to yelling.

Centers for Disease Control and Prevention. (2019, November). *Creating Rules.* Retrieved from

https://www.cdc.gov/parents/essentials/structure/rules.html

Positive Parenting Solutions. (n.d.). One Simple Phrase That Will Change Your Parenting Mindset Forever. Retrieved from https://www.positiveparentingsolutions.com/one-simple-phrase-change-parenting-mindset-forever

Cited for: Parenting mindset shift, "have to" vs. "get to" concept, positive reframing in parenting.

Happiest Baby. (n.d.). How to Keep Your Cool When Your Toddler Pushes Your Buttons. Retrieved from

https://www.happiestbaby.com/blogs/toddler/keep-your-cool-with-toddler